STRESS BREAKERS

BY HELENE LERNER
WITH ROBERTA ELINS

Illustrations by Pete Bastiansen

CompCare Publishers   2415 Annapolis Lane   Minneapolis, Minnesota 55441

Lerner, Helene, 1946-
  Stress breakers.

  Includes index.
  1. Stress (Psychology) I. Elins, Roberta.
II. Hesse, Bonnie B. III. Title.
BF575.S75L37   1985   158′.1   85-17509
ISBN 0-89638-074-2

Cover and interior design by Jeremy Gale

Inquiries, orders and catalog requests should be addressed to
CompCare Publishers
2415 Annapolis Lane
Minneapolis, Minnesota 55441
Call toll free 800/328-3330
(Minnesota residents 612/559-4800)

CompCare Publishers   2415 Annapolis Lane   Minneapolis, Minnesota 55441

           5   6   7
          88   89   90

WHAT'S IN THIS BOOK

Special thanks to Bonnie Hesse, who edited *Stress Breakers* with resourcefulness and imagination, perspective and insightful sensitivity to the language.

Thanks, too, to Leo Ramm, Brian Gardner, Jane Noland, Lila and Max K. Lerner for their encouragement; Roberta Elins, whose sense of humor diffused my stress; and Pam Bernstein who brought new life to my words. Many thanks also to Peggy Messina and Eleanor Pareres.

To all those wonderful people that this book can be of service to.
Helene Lerner

For Gary, with love.
Roberta Elins

When one glance at your computerized wristwatch tells you it's later than you think, you're a day behind schedule, your pulse is too fast, and you're overdrawn at the bank – you feel bombarded!

When the a.m. anchorman announces the news – another military crisis heats up, the stock market is down, and your favorite team lost again – then wishes you "good day," you wonder just how good a day it's going to be. And you feel bombarded!

When you've piloted carpools, paid off repairmen, folded stacks of laundry, squeezed in a teacher's conference and an exercise class before making dinner – only to have each member of your family get a separate invitation out by 5:00 – you renew your resolve to go back to college next quarter. And you bet you feel bombarded!

What do you do with all this stress? Don't blow up or break down. Break through...

             ... with *Stress Breakers.*

WHAT ARE STRESS BREAKERS?

Tongue-tied or talking too much? Frustrated or indecisive? On edge or downright outraged – often at inappropriate times? Most likely the cause is stress. A certain amount of stress is good; it's a challenge and a motivator. But enough is enough! And too much can lead to dangerous emotional and physical imbalances. That's when you need Stress Breakers – quick, portable techniques and tags of wisdom, all designed to ease the tension in your everyday life.

As a child, you took your "stress breaks" naturally. When you felt antsy, you raced around and wore out your restlessness. When you were fretful, you fell asleep. When you were grumpy, you went off by yourself until you felt tranquil again.

You restored your equilibrium intuitively because you didn't resist taking whatever calming action was necessary. You weren't in the prison of adulthood, sentenced to a stress term by words like "should," "have to," "hurry up," and "everybody." You gave yourself permission to take an intermission.

Now, as an adult, you have to re-learn to relax.

Before beginning, understand that the first and most crucial step is *awareness*. You must grasp the simple, but key concept that you are stressed because you are stressable. That is, *it is your reaction to a situation that stresses you, not the situation itself.*

Take the express lane at the grocery store, for example. The guy in front of you who has ten items too many and wants to write a check – very slowly – doesn't cause your stress. *You* do. Don't agree? Check your feelings. How do you feel when you're behind this slow-motion shopper and you're late for a dinner date? How do you feel when you're mulling over a heady compliment from your boss while you wait?

Now re-read that key principle: *your reaction, not the situation, determines the stress you feel.*

3

Being aware of your emotional-physical self means understanding that you have a choice about the way you feel. And you can learn to take charge of your reactions. A powerful ally in this effort is your own sense of humor. Laughter is a natural release. Its restorative powers come highly recommended. Dr. William Fry of Stanford University calls it "internal jogging." Norman Cousins watched re-runs of his favorite old slapstick comedies and literally laughed himself well from a serious illness.

The Stress Breakers in this book are sound but often deceptively simple physical and psychological exercises. Sometimes, as Dr. Toni Grant said, "Psychological exercises seem silly, but they do work!" How do we know? Because they are based on biophysical principles which are measurable in a clinical setting.

What causes *you* the most stress? A group of corporate executives were surveyed and their answers compared with a group of homemakers. The results were amazingly similar. Anger was the unanimous first response for both. Next were the constant interruptions, the inescapable telephone, the relentless tide of new work to do, and the never-finished feeling. These are just some of the universal stressors which can make anyone feel like a balloon blown up too tight and ready to pop.

So, what can you do? Stop – if only for a moment – and take time for a stress break.

Stress Breakers are divided into three groups: specific ways of coping with that super stressmaker of all time – anger, pick-me-up techniques that bring quick relief for the unpredictable tension times, and lifelong allies to help you through the perennial problems.

Ready to read on? You have nothing to lose – except those headaches, tight muscles, knotted stomachs, and feelings of frustration and helplessness.

YOU'RE STRESSED BECAUSE YOU'RE STRESSABLE.

STRESS BREAKERS

For That Super Stressmaker: Anger

THE ANGER AFFLICTION

Anger almost always brings stress unless you become a pro at letting go. When the guy who's been tailgating for ten minutes finally passes and then slows down in front of you, irritation is a natural response. But check your feelings: Are your feathers mildly ruffled, or are you in such a rage that you tailgate *him* to get even? Then ask yourself this: Is the tailgater the only target of your hostility, or is it open season on the highway? The "what's your hurry?" senior citizen, the lane-changing trucker, the teenager bebopping to her radio's rock beat – are they compatriots on the commuter trail or offenders impeding your progress? Honest answers to these questions will give you an indication of the intensity of your anger affliction.

Taking charge of anger, as with any emotion, begins with awareness. When you're storming or in a stew, don't dwell on what you'd like to call someone, zero in on how you feel. Stop and admit: "I'm angry."

Next, understand that anger is *not* bringing about a change for the better in the circumstances you're angry about. Giving a driver the international high sign seldom makes him apologetic and cooperative. Yelling at your daughter for painting her punk haircut purple rarely gets the response. "You're right, Mom, Dad. How could I so thoughtlessly embarrass you by following such a foolish fad!"

Even after you have accurately labeled your anger and understood its futility, the question remains: how to get rid of the churning? The final step is to take action. These action-oriented Stress Breakers are tailor-made for the Anger Affliction.

The "Down and Out" Simmer-down

In a nutshell, put your anger down and get it out. That is, ventilate your wrath by writing about it. Set aside a special notebook in a handy place – slide it in the top drawer of your desk or in among your phone books. When anger engulfs you, pick up a pen and begin to write. Don't plan what to say – spill it out. Don't analyze or organize – just pour your feelings on the paper.

Keep writing until you have nothing more to say to the maddening person or about the irritating situation. You'll know when you've said enough because you'll feel lighter and released. The act of writing is a process which literally lets the emotion flow from your body through your pen, down and out onto the paper.

Coincidental with the "pour your anger through your pen" process is another phenomenon: the writing seems to clear the air of the smoke and fumes of your anger, unclouding your vision and restoring your perspective. Just how important is the issue you're angry about? If it is important, is anger going to solve the problem or get in the way of the solution?

ANGER: DON'T PEN IT IN, PEN IT OUT!

The Big Burn Burn-off

For the slow-burning or the flagrantly consumed, a necessary final step to writing down and ridding yourself of the anger is to rip out those pages you've spilled your anger on and destroy them. Burn them ceremoniously. Or stomp them, shred them, scatter them over a garbage dump. These are symbolic actions which, combined with physical energy spent doing them, maximize the emotional release.

Anger Absorber

Just as the famous Jerusalem "wailing wall" receives the grievous ravings of those who cry before it, your own angry emotions can be absorbed in a natural setting.

For example, the ocean can be an outlet for you. As you stand before the pounding surf, open your hands and stretch them out straight toward the crashing curls. Place the anger in your palms and it will be sucked away from you into the receding, retreating, whispering foam. Letting your anger be absorbed in this way brings release and relief.

Fast Motion (the Noiseless Scream)

Though screaming anger out is popular therapy, sometimes it would
bring the paddy wagon or warp your child for life. In that case try
Fast Motion. Strike out at the classic punching bag. Toss around
a medicine ball. Or take to a jogging path and run off your wrath.

To you househusbands or housebound mothers and wives,
trapped by circumstances and suffering from four-walls fever, attack the floors with a
scrub brush, wash down your ceilings, vacuum vigorously. Feel your anger melt away.
Fast Motion is the equivalent of a scream with no noise.

Whether you make a lot of noise or none, the process is the same.
Physical action vents emotion.

White Lighting

This technique is specially designed for parents, particularly parents of teenagers.
Adolescence is a strange condition, for those who've got it don't know they have it. All
they know is that they have an unnatural love of mirrors and an urgent need to to do
the opposite of what you ask.

As your most (and least) favorite young person enters the room, before you read
the little darling the riot act for a) the missing car keys, b) the parking ticket, c) the
fridge door left standing open, d) the pile of wet towels in the bathroom, and e) the
mangled state of your make-up stick, which you need to color over the circles under
your eyes and your teen borrows routinely to camouflage zits – stop and consider.
Before you recite this standard list of adolescent wrongs, imagine a white light, an
aura, around your child. Then name all the things you love best – his impish grin, her
glorious smile, the innocent years, the close and comfortable times. Feel the

tension begin to subside, absorbed into the wonderful white light, Now you can address your grievances in a calm and rational manner.

White Lighting works its wonders if you have conflicts with other loved ones too, especially spouses. When you are ready to put aside your own need to be angry, illuminate the love of your life in white light. Then imagine all the good reasons he or she had for what happened. Your anger dissolves rapidly when you understand why the conflict occurred.

To summarize, the prescription for overcoming anger has three ingredients: awareness, understanding, and then action. And when it comes to action, if what you're doing doesn't work, do something else. Otherwise, pent-up anger can turn into rage and the spilling of Mt. St. Helen's will seem like a small-town Fourth of July picnic compared to your explosion!

**Rx FOR ANGER:
AWARENESS, UNDERSTANDING, ACTION.**

STRESS BREAKERS

Quick Pick-me-ups

POSITIVE PEPTALKS

If you think about it, on any given day the person you talk to most is yourself! This silent, one-way conversation may range from commenting on the weather to encouraging yourself in the face of a difficult task.

What you say to yourself can make the difference between creating tension and helping you cope with stress in a productive manner. In other words, the voice within can be your best cheerleader or a never-satisfied critic.

By using your thoughts in a positive, encouraging way, you can break this cycle:

So what you want to do is change your Negative Chatter – destructive, immobilizing mind talk – into Positive Peptalks.

No More Negative Chatter!

The first step is to become aware that you do indeed engage in Negative Chatter. For example, when you wake up to three feet of snow and your car is a gargantuan cupcake, you finally dig it out and the battery's dead, then "Gee, it's a great day!" probably will not be your first thought.

The chatter runs like a negative commentary from what Dr. Christian Schriner calls your "Internal Problem Finder." Most of the time you're unconscious of this personal diatribe which affects your whole being, but you can train yourself to stop it.

Check your thoughts throughout the day, especially when you're feeling angry or depressed. Stop what you're doing and take a look at what you're telling yourself. It's probably some slur at yourself that only makes the problem worse: "How could I be such a (ninny, dumbell, fool, clod, turkey, etc.)?" "What a stupid mistake!"

Knowing you have negative thoughts can lead to choosing constructive ones instead. Whenever you hear yourself saying, "I can't...I won't...I don't" – STOP! Re-think the sentence and substitute "I can...I will...I do!"

The hard part of rechanneling Negative Chatter into positive thinking is to *continue* spotting negativity and changing it. Keep practicing and don't get discouraged.

Here are some common stress collectors with constructive alternatives:

NEGATIVE CHATTER	CONSTRUCTIVE ALTERNATIVES
I can't do it . . . I've never done it before.	Doing something new is frightening, but exciting too. I don't have to do it perfectly the first time.
They're not here yet. They must be in an accident. I'll start calling the hospitals.	They're late. There must be a logical reason. Traffic is slow at this time of day.
This is a beautiful dress, and I look awful in it. I wish I were more attractive.	This is a beautiful dress – for somebody. It's not right for me. I'll keep on looking till I find what I need.
I'll never be able to handle all the extra work that goes with my promotion.	I often feel this way when beginning something new. I need to remember that my previous work performance earned me this promotion. I'm building on success.

Another hint to help you choose positive thoughts is to *accept what cannot be changed*.

"I'm five-feet-two – I'll never be tall!"

"I'll never be Queen of England."

"I can't stay young forever."

Unless you're ten years old and still growing, Princess Di, or the hero of a novel, these are all statements that are irrevocably true! When you feel sorry for yourself because of what you *don't* have, look at what you *do*.

Mirror Talk

At night when you're ready to fold up and fall in bed, as you stand there in front of the mirror, eyes glazed, mechanically brushing your teeth, there's a good possibility that your Internal Problem Finder is still having a field day, busily feeding you a line of Negative Chatter. "You didn't do this... you didn't do that... there are mountains of should-have-dones that you didn't do today."

To break this practice, force yourself out of your slough of regrets. Focus on your image in the mirror. Now recollect and repeat what you *did* do today. "Paid bills, straightened out the insurance matter, fixed the leaky faucet, etc." Unless you had a day off, you'll discover that you actually accomplished a great deal. You *did* more than you *didn't*.

Then why are you listing the negatives instead of the positives? Maybe it's because you have a die-hard tendency to put yourself down. In that case, your next line probably will be, "I may have done a lot, but I should have done more." This, of course, discounts your accomplishments and implies that you've never done enough until you've done it *all*. What you're really saying is, "If I don't do *everything* – and, what's more, do it perfectly – I'm not okay and not worthy."

If this is one of your credos, be careful – there's a lot of stress pressed between the lines. Do you really expect to be able to do everything? If so, you're wasting energy. No one can do Everything. It's not possible to be Perfect. People who strive for a limitless goal spend most of their lives coming up short and feeling bad about it.

20

To estimate whether your overall orientation is positive or negative, take this simple test: Look at a glass partly filled with water – is it half empty or half full? If your immediate response is "half empty," chances are your outlook is primarily pessimistic and your self-esteem is out of shape. Exercise your right to change those negative perceptions and break the stress they bring.

Another reason people sometimes take a pessimistic point of view is simply out of habit. Someone said, "First we make our habits – then our habits make us." Dr. David Viscott said, "You live your attitude."

Maybe you learned criticism from chronic criticizers as a child. Maybe you let yourself slide into the pits by not recognizing or examining Negative Chatter. Putting yourself down – for your appearance, physical fitness, mental outlook, economic or artistic achievement, or whatever – is never fun or funny. It's stressful.

But take heart and take hold. Don't be hard on yourself for being hard on yourself. You've done enough of that already. Instead, be happy that you've made some important new discoveries and have a chance to re-orient yourself right now.

Look in the mirror and have a positive, heart-to-heart talk with *you*.

MIRROR, MIRROR ON THE WALL...
AM I BEING FAIR TO MYSELF AT ALL?

NEGATIVE THOUGHTS ARE ENERGY BURNERS.
POSITIVE THOUGHTS ARE ENERGY EARNERS.

Life Savers

In addition to ridding your mind of Negative Chatter, when in distress learn to throw yourself a Life Saver, a simple, positive saying which has meaning for you and brings immediate support. Life Savers are phrases that have worked for you before; repeating them to yourself generates feelings of calm – something like grabbing for a security blanket.

Some classic lines which have worked for many people are:

Easy does it, but do it...

One step at a time.

First things first.

What are my priorities?

Keep it simple.

I choose life.

A Life Saver also can be a comment in someone else's voice cheering you on. Close your eyes and call upon a memory of encouragement: your husband congratulating you on a promotion... your teammates saying, "You can do it!"... your children saying, "You look handsome, Daddy." When self-doubt and worry begin, call upon a Life Saver.

Think of life-saving phrases that have given you strength in the past and write them down. Then, in addition, make up five more that you would like to try out. Memorize them so you'll have immediate recall.

LIFE SAVERS

GOOD OLD BUOYS   NEW PORTS

1. _____   1. _____

2. _____   2. _____

3. _____   3. _____

4. _____   4. _____

5. _____   5. _____

Read over your list of Life Savers regularly, adding to them as you live. Concentrate on the good feelings they bring.

WHEN YOU'RE DROWNING IN DISTRESS, THROW YOURSELF A LIFE SAVER.

YOU DON'T HAVE TO SINK. THINK — POSITIVELY!

TENSION TAMERS

Taming tension simply means re-learning to relax, an ability which Dr. Herbert Benson of Harvard University assures us we're all born with. The "relaxation response," according to Dr. Benson, is ours for the doing. Probably the biggest obstacle is convincing ourselves to take the time to do it.

You Deserve a Stress Break Today

Lunch is a perfect time to replenish your inner resources with a stress break. Whenever possible, leave whatever you're doing and get up and go. If you work in an office, keep a pair of walking shoes in a desk drawer. When high noon hails others to calories and conversation, don your health habit and stride out for a brisk walk. Don't meander, saunter, or stroll. Stride out briskly, arms swinging, legs stretching, breath flowing in and out, in and out.

A fifteen-minute walk, with sharpened awareness of breathing, movement, and motion, will bring you back to the office invigorated and renewed.

If you are a professor with a pillar of papers to grade or a graduate student with an overcrowded brain, don't hide, stride. You too deserve a stress break today.

RE-LEARN TO RELAX.

The Ready-mixed Refresher

If physical movement is an impossibility due to soggy or too-crisp weather, cramped quarters, or other circumstances beyond your control, go for the Ready-mixed Refresher – a professionally prepared relaxation cassette tape. Many excellent ones are now on the market. You can listen to nature's soothing sounds (an owl, a whippoorwill, the slosh of an ocean) or to another person telling you gently to relax your mind and body, part by part.

First, get ready. Comfortable chair, feet up, headphones on, "Do not disturb" sign on your door. Inhale deeply. Exhale slowly. Begin the tape – and begin to feel peaceful.

The Allowing Attitude

From acupuncture to deep-breath kung fu, from meditation to massage, the techniques and philosophies of Eastern cultures have always been light years ahead of ours when it comes to mind over stressful matters. Think of the serenity in the timeless simplicity of oriental symbols – sand, rock, and age-old bonsais.

To let go of your own tension, try an adaptation of an ancient T'ai chi exercise. Settle yourself in a quiet place. Interlock your fingers as if to pray. Point your index fingers upward, leaving space between them. Study the space between them, then allow them to come together. Don't push them together. Allow them to close slowly on their own. (A measure of your tension is how hard it can be to hold those fingers apart. Do they want to snap shut?)

Open them again and feel the breath of your emotions escape through the opening. Then name your stresses. Did your candidate lose the election? Has the IRS demanded an audit? Is your first-born leaving the nest without ceremony? You can't change those things, so let the destructive tension go. Watch the stressful feelings flow out through your open fingers. Then allow them quietly, peacefully, tranquilly to close.

There is so much in our lives we can't control. Dr. Robert Eliot of the University of Nebraska says, "If you can't fight and you can't flee, flow." And let go.

Hug Therapy

The most natural form of stress release is the touch of another human being. When you were very young, you hollered for help and ran for mother. When you marched boldly into first grade, you probably held tight to her hand to give you courage.

Whatever your age, your need to touch and be touched is the same. Whether you're fearful or uptight, sad or angry, a heartfelt hug can do wonders to ease the uncomfortable feelings.

If you're very lucky, you have a trusted lover, spouse, or special friend you can ask for "a hug, please." (But don't wait for your hugger to guess your need. You are responsible for taking action!)

Even if you don't know a person intimately, you still can reach out for a hello or good-bye squeeze, a hug or a handshake. Just the process of reaching out has its own rewards.

If right at this moment a part of your stress is the lack of someone to hug, there are common interest or common need groups who can support you with open arms and hearts.

Also, don't discount pets as de-stressors. A pet can be a wonderfully cozy, dependable companion, offering unconditional love and allowing hugs as needed. Sitting in a soft chair stroking a cat or patting a dog is soothing to the spirit and restores the soul.

Nature Does Wonders

Nature in its vastness (the breadth of sky or prairie) and its elegant detail (the perfection of a miniature wildflower, just shoe high) is a calming resource.

Look – really look – at a pond with its lily pads and water spiders. Or carefully contemplate a tree. Notice the texture of the bark (touch it), the lift of the branches, the flow of the leaf patterns. If you're agile and the tree is low-branching, climb up and sit in the lap of a sturdy limb. Listen to the leaves. You'll be amazed at the energy and comfort you will find if you allow a tree to be a Tension Tamer.

Just becoming part of a natural scene for a while can give you the serene sense of belonging to a wider universe beyond the piques of everyday stress.

Quiet Coves

Did you know that relaxation imagery is a vital part of the training of world-class athletes, including many in the United States and the Soviet Union? Baseball teams hire consulting psychologists to guide their pitchers through relaxation exercises before working out. Believe it or not, most of these pitchers' "earned run averages" drop dramatically, proving once again that taking time to relax, to break stress, improves a person's overall performance.

One way to be your own relaxation therapist is to imagine the place where you feel most peaceful and keep a picture of it nearby – on your desk, refrigerator door, dashboard, or stuck in the edge of your mirror – wherever you occasionally glance. And grab hold of a peaceful feeling.

For some people the scene is a tropical cove or a tide-smoothed beach at dawn. For others it's a meadow with a meandering stream or the strong shoulders of a mountain range. Still others will picture peace in the varnished tables of the public library or the stained glass window in a chapel. Whatever you are instinctively drawn to is the picture for you.

THE THREE R's OF STRESS BREAKING: REST, RELAX, REGENERATE.

Keys and Cues

Similar to keeping a peaceful picture nearby is to have a cue word which conjures up a calm feeling for you. This is an important technique with big personal pay-offs. Begin this Stress Breaker by reconstructing a time when you felt terrific – when your self-esteem was high and your anxiety low:

- After a hiatus from academia – ten years of child-bearing and child-tending – you just opened your first graduate school report card and discovered all A's!
- Your business partner credited you with landing a huge account and you were able to tell him you had just clinched another, even bigger deal!
- You awoke one February morning expecting to feel wintry and awful; instead, it smelled like spring outside, the sun warmed your back, people who seldom smiled smiled – and euphoria followed you around all day.

Reconstruct this grand time in your mind's eye and feel those feelings again. Catch them, relive them, then find a key word or phrase to name them. Any one- or two-word label will do, preferably the first that comes to mind. Got it? Now, with practice, you can condense the process, key into the good times, and call up the pleasant feelings *on cue* with your word association.

Preparing for a big speech? Ready to tee off in a golf tournament? The Cub Scout pack about to descend? Recall, on cue, those key words that bring serenity and support.

WATCH YOUR KEYS AND CUES.

CREATIVE TALKING PICTURES

How you "see" your life, your job, and your relationships influences how you will act in a situation. We have all been trained in this visual age that "seeing is believing," "a picture is worth a thousand words," and "what you see is what you get."

Each of us is equipped with an internal camera, a mind's eye, which creates mental pictures – movies of the mind. Using the Stress Breaker called Creative Talking Pictures, you can empower yourself through visualization.

Creative Talking Pictures, unlike the movies you see in the theater, are films in which you're the director, producer, and star. Make them reflect what you want out of life.

You Oughta Be in Pictures

When there is a difficult project to complete, picture your supervisor praising you for a job well done. Feeling positive about yourself and your abilities makes it easier to get to work. Optimism always improves the chances for success.

When you're anxious about a tennis game with a new partner, visualize yourself relaxed and steady, playing with authority and a smile on your face. The principle here is the self-fulfilling prophecy – the idea that expecting a particular result can bring about that result.

We all have the power to create these positive images. The key is to use your imagination constructively. Fantasies based on imagining the very worst that can happen will only lead to frustration, but a Talking Picture with a good, old-fashioned happy ending is a positive exercise. Take the following example:

Your little girl has just left for her first day of school. Because you're feeling nervous, you imagine her to be afraid, crying, or even the unthinkable – running away, out the school doors, and getting lost on the way home.

STOP

Visualize your daughter eagerly raising her hand in class, playing games at recess, then coming home with the name of her new best friend and her first piece of art work.

Whether the "star" of your mental movie is you or someone you love, by creating a positive picture, you also create good feelings and reduce anxiety and stress.

Re-runs

Many times for many reasons, relationships don't run smoothly. Or the response you get from others is not 'what you want. Take this morning... A shouting match with your sixteen-year-old drained the energy you'd planned to use on a creative project today. Or your husband/wife left for work in a huff. Your first inclination at such prickly moments is to blame the other person. But the stressful feelings are yours, so check out the situation. Here's how: re-run the video tape of this morning's activities, but step out of the screen and join the audience.

You re-hash and rehearse the audio tracks of mental tapes quite regularly. ("Boy, next time she says that, I'm going to say this!") You can replay the video tracks of your tapes too.

So settle back in your seat and watch the re-run of this morning's breakfast time. Was there a smile on your face or a frown? Were your shoulders back in a positive posture, or were you slumping over your coffee, nose so close to the cup that there was steam on your face?

When your teen son asked for his agreed-upon allowance, did you say, brightly, "Here you are. Have a good day."? Or did you, wordlessly and grudgingly, shove the money across the table in his direction? When your spouse said, "How about dinner out tonight?" did you look up smile: "Great idea!" or did you continue cuddling your coffee cup and mutter, "Okay, if you want to"?

Watching yourself in action provides valuable information which allows you to make choices about how you act and what you say. If you aren't getting the response you want or being the person you want to be, then re-write the script for tomorrow morning.

Ready to step back into the screen? Shoulders back, head up. Giving your personal best is always an Oscar performance. And the winner is... you!

The Critic's Review

The Critic's Review technique is for advanced stress-relief, personal-improvement students only, so take heed. When you seem to be out of sorts or out of sync with others, find a trustworthy, candid person to act as your committed listener. Remembering that all anyone can know about you is what he or she hears or sees, ask for feedback on your behavior. "Our mutual friend says I seem aloof and uninvolved. What do you think?"

Growing up as part of a family, you probably got more feedback on your behavior than you wanted, no doubt a blow-by-blow accounting from parents and siblings as well. What you may not have known was that your Automatic Processor assimilated this information and made some adjustments accordingly. Something like this:

Sis: *"You are so gross I can't even believe it!"*
Mom: *"You really shouldn't bite your nails, dear."*
Automatic Processor: *"Hmmmm, constant nail-biting gets a bad reaction and isn't socially acceptable.*

Such conclusions are seldom voiced out loud – perhaps not verbalized at all; your Automatic Processor often operates on a non-verbal level.

Unfortunately, few adults are comfortable with criticism. So, when you invite your caring critic for an evaluation, be careful or it may dissolve into an old "I Love Lucy" routine:

> *"How do you like my new dress, Ricky?"*
> *"I don't like it."*
> *"I told you not to say that...Waaaah!"*

If the response you get from your critic is radically different from what you expect, ask another. But if both responses are the same and you still disagree, chances are your Processor is shut down and your Denial Screen is up. For some important reasons, known only to you and perhaps hidden down deep, you aren't willing to acknowledge some piece of reality. And so to protect yourself, you deny or discount the information.

To dismantle the Denial Screen, try to imagine possible ways your critics' feedback could be right. Ask your listeners for concrete behavioral clues to back up their reactions. "What did you see? What did you hear? How did that make you feel? Why?"

This exercise can be tough, but hopefully the risk and effort will be commensurate with the gain. Still, you have to be sincere in your intentions and highly motivated to reduce your stress. Want to try it? Good luck!

WILL YOU ACCEPT THE STATUS QUO? OR DO YOU WANT TO LEARN AND GROW?

Animal Answers

Every animal has his or her own personality. One fine Amazon parrot named Sam spends every day free, roaming the house. Just before his human friends come home from work, Sam goes into his cage and closes the door, pretending that he spent the whole day quietly in his cage being a "good" bird. Only the scattered birdseed gives him away.

Here's an exercise involving animals designed to ease a particular mental dilemma by tapping the creative side of your brain.

Pick an animal that you have a special feeling for – from tenderness to awe. The animal can be your own comfortable lap cat, a brilliant tiger, or a mythological griffon – a creation of your own imagination. Close your eyes and "see" a precise mental picture of your animal. Notice its color, shape, size, and textures.

Now choose a peaceful setting – sylvan, seaside, or something different – and walk to meet your animal there. Once you come within speaking distance, ask your animal the question which you've been struggling to answer and wait quietly for the response.

Usually the answer is immediate and clear and has come from the creative, emotional rather than the logical, intellectual side of you. How do you know it's your answer? You wrote the script, didn't you? The imaginary animal was merely a vehicle to reach your own deepest feelings about the issue.

So when practical reasoning fails and your lists of pros and cons lead nowhere, consult your canary or talk it over with your tiger – and put an end to the stress of indecision.

Look on the Other's Side

Now that you've sharpened your creative powers, you'll probably find it easier to understand what motivates another person. Use the ability to neutralize the stress in your relationships.

Whether you're a homemaker or the president of a large corporation, your power with people is based on being sensitive to their needs. By envisioning how someone is feeling at a particular time, you can gear your reactions to be helpful instead of intrusive. Like Jean B. did in this case:

> Jean B. has a client who is on his telephone when she enters his office. She hears that he's talking with his wife about their son, who is very sick. Jean is also a mother and can understand his distress. Although she has come with an important proposal, she tells him that the work can wait and instead talks about his son. Jean will present her idea at another time and is more likely to win his support.

Another useful time to Look on the Other's Side is when you are dealing with an out-and-out adversary. No one likes to admit to having adversaries, but we all do! It's hard to deal effectively with a person who disturbs you. One hospital administrator imagines a particularly trying member of her staff on a picnic with his family. When she does, her anger dissipates, and she can communicate with him more productively. Try this technique:

See the person who's upsetting you playing with children, petting the family dog, buying flowers on a street corner. Or inject a little human humor into your visuals – imagine her riding an elephant or him learning to roller skate, pratfalls and all. Imagining such acts of kindness or minicomedies will soften your attitude toward your adversary and shrink your stress.

> Every morning as he walked to work through a city office center, a certain young bank teller stopped to buy a cup of coffee from an embittered old vendor behind a counter. The young man consistently smiled and said, "Good morning," but there was never even a grunt in response. When asked about why he continued to be pleasant, the teller answered, "Why not? He probably has some good reasons to be bitter. Besides, why should I let *him* determine how I feel?"

It's never totally possible or even desirable to be unaffected by others, but when you're faced with a person who's difficult or a downer, a Look on the Other's Side will help you achieve what you want and make your everyday life more pleasant.

ENERGIZERS

What do you do when...

- the air conditioning on the commuter train breaks down again and neither you nor your seersucker suit is drip dry?
- it's eight o'clock and you're getting dressed for a black-tie party; your tuxedo isn't in the closet – it's at the cleaners, which closed an hour ago?
- you're writing a report for your manager who will determine whether or not the project you've been working on for eight months will be cut (along with the rest of your services) from next year's budget?
- your rent is due and your roommate spent her share on a bowling ball for her boyfriend?
- you have a flat on the freeway driving to the most important job interview of your life?
- you just slammed the phone down on your wife (husband, lover, friend, mother, child)?

Do you clench your fists? Bite your fingernails? Curl your toes? Twist your hair? Take antacids? All of the above? Now is the time to take a stress break instead.

You can do this by practicing the Stress Breaker exercises called Energizers, ever ready relief techniques that involve deep breathing. Breathing comes before food in the hierarchy of human needs. It is literally the force of life. Learn to breathe deeply and "the force will be with you."

So when stress threatens, instead of giving up or getting even, get Energized.

The Cosmic Breath

Close your eyes and relax your facial muscles. Begin to breathe deeply as you count down slowly from ten to one. Pay attention to the long inhalations and exhalations of your breath. Feel your stomach going OUT as you inhale and IN when you exhale. Notice the air flowing through your nose.

How can you remember to breathe deeply – instead of holding your breath – in the middle of a crisis? One way is to keep a cue card (BREATHE!) in sight – on the desk, refrigerator, steering wheel – wherever you can count on encountering stress. Once you make this Stress Breaker a part of your life, you'll use it automatically.

Max is an attorney in his early sixties who is constantly on the go. He uses deep breathing when stress mounts up during the day. At the onset of a crisis, he breathes deeply and takes a short walk.

"After my alone time, I feel refreshed and ready to meet the next challenge."

There is nothing mysterious about the Cosmic Breath energizer. It gives you time to diffuse your anger or alleviate your anxiety and focuses you on something other than your stress. It also can lower your heart rate and tension level. Before going to bed is an ideal time to practice this technique.

So the next time your boss thinks you're less than brilliant, your wife's chicken cordon bleu is noir (charred black), or you want to put the kids up for adoption, don't blast out – breathe in!

CHECK YOUR FEELINGS. ARE YOU IN CHARGE?

The Brief Breather

If you're into a mid-day slump and need a quick pick-me-up, take three short in-and-out breaths followed by a long inhalation and exhalation. You'll break the fatigue cycle and feel more lively.

Peace Time for Passengers

At 11:00 a.m. on a dash to a business meeting on the other side of town, sit in the cab, close your eyes and relax your facial muscles. Feel your back rest against the seat. Then begin consciously to inhale and exhale for a few minutes. At the end of the ride you will feel refreshed and composed. You can unreel on wheels in a cab, bus, train, or back seat of a car. This will work for an on-the-move executive, a student heading for a final exam, even for a parent on the way to a PTA meeting if she or he can just once get out of the driver's seat. (Is a parent ever a passenger?)

The Instant Pacer

Take a minute to close your eyes and *become aware of your physical state.* Are you empty and tired? Or are you brimming with energy? Don't resist the way you're feeling. If you are tired, take a five-minute cat nap. Close the door, recline in a comfortable chair, and close your eyes. You're not wasting time; you have the right to rest. Besides, revitalizing yourself will make you more productive when you return to your task.

If you are an executive whose days consist of making decisions and attending meetings, cocktail parties, and business dinners – or a busy parent whose children range from toddlers to teens – or a student juggling classes, dating, and an after-school job, you can maintain maximum effectiveness by practicing these Energizers.

GIVE YOURSELF PERMISSION TO TAKE AN INTERMISSION.

YOU HAVE THE RIGHT TO REST.

STRESS SEARCH

Have you ever gone to your doctor complaining of the blues or the blahs, only to be told there's nothing physically wrong? You probably leave that doctor's office confused – even a little angry. You still hurt, and you don't know why or what to do about it.

Stress may begin in the mind, but it announces itself, sometimes very loudly, in the body. Our bodies have a way of rebelling against too much pressure. Those inexplicable aches and pains, that consuming sense of fatigue, are most often tension-induced.

After becoming aware that you are stressed, the next step in stress-breaking is the Stress Search. Where, exactly, does your body rebel? Neck, back, stomach? Discover where your stress points are and you'll know what area to work on with the exercises which follow.

FIND YOUR STRESS POINTS

Check off your stress points on the inventory below. Although the situations may not be exactly like yours, they will help you identify the symptoms described.

STRESS SYMPTOM	STRESS MAKER
The throbbing headache	It's wonderful being mom, wife, head chauffeur, scrubperson, and hostess, but when your thirteen-year-old calls you an airhead and your third grader volunteers you and your house for the class Christmas party, that's when the pounding begins.

Continued

43

STRESS SYMPTOM	STRESS MAKER
The furrowed forehead	The pressure of too much to do makes you scrunch up your brow. But you know that stress is taking its toll when you relax your face and it looks like the drawing in a paint-by-number kit.
The tic	At a staff meeting of the company you recently joined, you finally get up the nerve to speak! As you open your mouth, you notice your supervisor staring at your right eye – which has begun to twitch uncontrollably.
Grinding teeth	You're twenty minutes late for the theater and stuck in a traffic jam. You try to speak to suggest another route – and your jaws are clamped shut so tight that the hinges hurt!
Dry throat	You're at a celebration dinner – in your honor – and the spoons on the glasses have announced your speech. You rise, try to form the words, but your throat is so dry that you couldn't talk even if you remembered what you'd planned to say.
The neck ache	Your fiancee has announced that she has accepted a medical scholarship in Spain and postponed the wedding date for two *more* years!
Hives	Your perfectionism leaves its spots. For every unreasonable demand you make on yourself, a hive appears on your body!
Handwaving	You're no longer capable of speaking and are gesturing like a traffic cop during rush hour.
Clammy hands	You've spent a fortune on a new outfit to impress your blind date. His appreciative look as you open the door tells you he's noticed. But your attempt at a poised meeting is foiled by your handshake – your hand is wet as a just-caught catfish.

STRESS SYMPTOM	STRESS MAKER
Foot-tapping, finger-drumming	You're marching (in place) to a stress drummer. At a money meeting with your auditors over lunch, your left foot is tapping like a woodpecker on the table base – when the base moves out from under your foot; it was your chief auditor's toe!
Stomach pain	You have pains as you realize that after spending $40,000 on your daughter's college education, she can't find a job because she's overqualified!
Lower back pain	You've chained yourself to your desk to finish an overdue report. When you finally get up, the weight is off your shoulders – but the pain is in your back!
Leg aches and shakes	You've planned the perfect wedding, down to the last detail. But as the organist launches into "Lohengrin," your legs are shaking so hard that you catch your heel in the hem of your dress.

When you've finished the Stress Search and have isolated points where you feel pressures, get in the habit of recording situations which cause stress – and your body's reactions to it – in a Stress Log like the sample on pages 96 and 97. For example, you might write, "Husband/wife complains that I haven't done my share of the housework this week – stomach ache." Or "Mother-in-law calls to say she's coming for a two-week visit at Christmas – stomach ache *and* headache."

Now, on to the next chapter for exercises designed to relax your body's Stress Points.

LET'S GET PHYSICAL

Think back to those physical symptoms of tension that you discovered in your Stress Search. Remember the fishy hands, the hives, aches, and kinks that bother your body just when you *need* all of your strength to cope with the stress that's causing the symptoms. The pains and knots center at your Stress Points, begging you to slow down. When tension makes you tight and stress puts the squeeze on you, it's time to get physical and loosen up.

Each stress point has its own unstressing exercise. Let's take it from the top...

STRESS-POINT STRESS BREAKERS

STRESS POINT: FACE. For nervous tics, furrowed brow, throbbing temples, or clenched jaw, try...

The Jaw Drop

Imagine lying on a quiet beach, being warmed by the sun and pillowed by the sand. Relax. Now open your mouth and drop your lower jaw slightly. Keep this position for ten seconds.

The Funny Face

Contort your face into an exaggerated mask, tightening your facial muscles. Hold your "funny face" for three seconds, then relax. Feel the tension melt away.

The Healing Hand

Close your eyes and locate the precise area of the throbbing or tightness. Place your finger on the area and apply light pressure.

STRESS POINT: NECK AND SHOULDERS. When you're stressed, pain in your neck and shoulders, caused by your muscles knotting up, is very common. Learn to give these aches the cold shoulder with...

Knot Openers

The next time you're tense, find out exactly where you feel the stress. If it's in your shoulders, tighten your arm and shoulder muscles, then release them. Repeat this five times to reduce the tension.

The Soft Touch

Gently rub your fingers back and forth over the tense area. Keep this up for as long as it takes to feel relief. Ask a friend to lend a hand or two. Don't be bashful; you'll return the favor when he or she needs it.

The Wheel Grip

When ordinary arm-and-shoulder tension is compounded by the stress of being stuck in traffic or by your immobility while driving long distances, grip your steering wheel tight – really tight – for a few seconds, then release it. This is a really useful loosener for drivers.

STRESS POINT: STOMACH AND LOWER BACK. These pains can occur in anyone at any time. Get relief with...

The Tum Tuck

Tuck in your stomach – tight – then release the tension. Do this three to five times. You'll find this works well when you're angry but you want to avoid an argument. A worthwhile bonus: while you're easing tension, you're trimming your middle.

The Circle Stroke

Stroke your stomach by gently making circles with the palm of your hand around the areas that ache. Ask a friend to take both palms and do the same for your lower back. This technique is sometimes used to help cranky babies fall asleep. It works just as well for a cranky adult.

FOR THE TOTAL BODY:

The Raggedy Ann Rag

Get rid of general body tension by imagining yourself as limp as Raggedy Ann (or Andy). To do this, sing yourself a rag-doll rag and jump in place for two minutes while you shake your arms and legs. There's an aim for all this floppiness: you'll be relaxed, limbered up, and ready for anything! (And remember, the words "I love you" are stitched near Raggedy Ann's heart. When you can say these words to someone, just feel the stress subside!)

FIGHT FATIGUE – GET PHYSICAL!

PLEASURIZERS

Stress-Point Stress Breakers sometimes will take out the kinks but won't chase the blues away. Life seems to have lost its sizzle and sparkle, and you need to discover some new Pleasurizers. Do something nice for yourself – maybe even something slightly extravagant. A little hedonism can be healthy!

The Enjoyment Mug

Instead of sitting down to a cup of coffee or tea, when you need a lift pour yourself a mug of pure enjoyment. The recipe is simple. Fill a cup with folded paper strips. On each strip write down something fabulous you would like to do or have already done. One friend adds to her mug promising horoscopes and slips from well-wishing fortune cookies. Each morning, pick a strip and refer to it during the day.

Goal-oriented Enjoyment Mugs can spur you on to greater achievements. On your desk at work, or in your home, fill the mug with positive slogans to challenge you ("you can do it!"), honor past accomplishments, ("winning the club golf trophy in 1964"), or spark excitement about an upcoming event ("a ski weekend" or "a reunion of classmates").

Just as coffee can become stale after a while, your Enjoyment Mug should be refilled every week or so to keep it fresh and full of new thoughts to bring you maximum pleasure.

Serene Sketching

Calm yourself by focusing on something or someone – preferably a serene subject – and sketching it. Tell your internal critic it's okay not to be Picasso, these drawings are for *you*. Some ideas for Serene Sketching:

- A tree – any tree in any season.
- An imaginary vacation retreat
- A portrait of the family cat or dog (bird, horse, gerbil, iguana, etc.)
- A bowl of apples
- A beautiful dress for your daughter to wear to the prom
- Your own abstract idea of peace

Painting, too, is a constructive outlet for negative emotions. Your dark mood can be expressed by slathering midnight colors on canvas. Paint swaths in broad brush strokes can represent your sweeping anger or enveloping gloom. Many psychic healers and psychologists believe that colors reflect and influence your mental state. Blue, for example, is thought to be a peaceful color, while red excites and energizes.

The Music Bath

Take a long soak in a hot tub, and wash away your tension. A shower is fine for getting the body clean, but when the spirit needs cleansing, nothing beats a warm, luxurious, drawn-out bath.

You may not have thought about a bath as a Pleasurizer, but this is no ordinary, hasty tubbing.

1. Plan to spend at least thirty minutes in the tub.

2. Take the phone off the hook. (One of the most high-stress moments of all of life's petty annoyances is summed up in the ringing phone, the leap out of the tub, the dripping, the chilling – and the picking up of the receiver to a dial tone and a vanished caller.)

3. Put on your favorite music-to-tub-by in a nearby room. Have a tape ready for just this purpose. If you don't have an appropriate cassette, sing or hum yourself a tranquil tune.

Oliver Wendell Holmes thought the music more essential than the water. He said, "Take a music bath once or twice a week... you will find that it is to the soul what the water is to the body." Most high-stress persons who have discovered this Pleasurizer prefer both – water *and* music – in combination.

When the world is too much with you and you feel like throwing in the towel, get out your thickest, most absorbent one instead – and run yourself a music bath. Even the small waterfall sound of the tub filling is a de-stressor!

Add to your own Pleasurizers. Remember to keep looking for small, pleasurable experiences to brighten your life as they lighten your load.

QUACK

STRESS BREAKERS

Lifelong Allies for Long-term Stress

HOW DO YOU TELL TIME?

In a world of fast lanes, fast food, and generally fast living, people are always playing "beat the clock" – a game no one can win. As we all know, clock-racing can result in a straitjacket of stress.

You can't stop time or speed it up. You can't make more time or recover lost time. What you *can* do is change how you feel about time. These feelings are important indicators of your stress level.

For starters, check your first response to this question: Does time feel like a friend or an enemy? If your answer is ambivalent, go a step further and make a mental image of time as an animal. Is it a large, menacing beast or is it a comfortable, benign, peaceful creature? When time feels like a threatening opponent, then a vague, free-floating sense of urgency probably crawls up and down your spine.

Next, listen to your language. How do you talk about time? Which of these signal phrases are part of your litany?

If I only had time...

There just aren't enough hours in the day!

Hurry up – we'll be late!

If you keep moving at that rate...!

In addition to these verbal clues, check something else that is very indicative of your sense of time – the way you drive. Which of the following describe your driving? Do you:

Pull out of your driveway at a rate that would make a parking attendant proud?
Approach a red light at full speed, then brake hard (screech!) to stop?
Lurch ahead – and beat the car next to you – when the light turns green?
Change lanes frequently so you can go faster?
Turn the air blue with your language (and you are not an off-road curser at all!)?

These simple indicators are designed to lift your awareness so you can make choices about your time-related stress level. After all, how can you take off a stress straitjacket unless you know you have one on?

YOU CAN'T BEAT THE CLOCK...
BUT YOU CAN STOP RACING TIME.

"Unclock Your Life"

When Dr. Larry Dossey of Dallas, Texas, said to "unclock your life," he meant to set aside the struggle against time, the futile, stressful effort to control the uncontrollable. While acknowledging the wisdom of this idea, we typically tense up and try harder to go slow and relax! We know what we're supposed to do, but, as simple as it sounds, for some reason we can't do it. As in Timothy Gallwey's "inner tennis" concept, we can be told how to hold our racquets, how to position our bodies, but still we struggle to perform, probably becoming even more stressed and frustrated because we don't know (or rather, can't remember) what a relaxed body looks and feels like. Our battles and tensions keep us from reaching our full potential, on the tennis court or anyplace else.

To help you reset your inner body clock to a peaceful pace, there are two good role models to watch – one who doesn't know what time is and one who understands very well the plodding march of time. Both are at the extremes of life's age spectrum – the very young and the very old.

Spend a morning with a small child. Notice how he moves, oblivious of time, paced only by natural and biological clocks. He wakes when it's light, sleeps when it's dark, eats when he's hungry instead of when the clock dictates that "it's time." Watch the child meander on a lawn or a sidewalk, stopping to examine whatever flags his interest, stooping or squatting to pick up a leaf or a stick or a caterpillar. Notice that when he wants to go fast, to catch up with others or to join in a game, he even hurries unstressfully!

Later the child will learn about bedtime, mealtime, school time, and being on time. For now, he is free of the tyranny of time – and free of the stress that time-watching brings.

Next, visit a woman who has lived for many years, who understands and uses expanses of time, for whom time itself is a source of pleasure. Her pace is slow and steady – no great bursts of energy, but purposeful progress instead. There is contentment in routine, and satisfaction comes in doing small things carefully and well.

The old woman enjoys each part of the day for the things which happen then, as opposed to marking time, waiting for what will happen later.

Notice the negative reactions of both the old woman and the child to being rushed; it's easy to see that conforming to clock time can create stress.

By observing them, learn for yourself what it means in body language to move purposefully but without the pressure of being driven by time's exigencies. These two, the elderly woman and the child, are released from the constraints of clock time. Be with such clock-free people when you can. Their calm and contentment can be contagious.

CLOCK-FREE IS STRESS-FREE.

Take Time Out

As a time-release Stress Breaker, take time out of your life each week – that is, literally remove it. Let your internal (and eternal) clock-watching vigilante take a short vacation. Remove or cover all visible signs of time. Unhang or swaddle your clocks. Take off your watch and put it in a drawer. Enjoy yourself, paced only by your natural rhythm, not by the imposition of the sixty-minute hour. If you have an appointment, date, or other necessary ending to this exercise, set an alarm. It will signal you when it's time to get back into time.

Another way to release yourself from clock-consciousness for awhile is to participate in an activity which causes you to lose your awareness of time. This Stress Breaker must be strictly individualized, but whatever the job, sport, or hobby, if you become so absorbed that you lose track of passing minutes or hours, you have been liberated for that period from the confinement of time. Make sure this activity is a regular part of your routine. It's one of the best Stress Breakers of all!

**TAKE TIME OUT OF YOUR LIFE.
TAKE TIME OUT _FOR_ YOUR LIFE.**

Future Pacing

Our everyday language is littered with references which reflect our conscious and unconscious preoccupation with time: uptime, downtime, advance time, production time, time-sharing, behind the time, timely (and untimely), test of time. How often at work do we hear phrases like "time is of the essence," or "timing is all-important." Such deference to time is enough to make time bombs of us all!

Most of us waste a good deal of energy trying to control time – especially future time. Somehow in our psyches, a logic link has slipped; a recognition that there is no control over tomorrow has shifted to an unacknowledged sense of urgency to try to grasp the time ahead and secure it safely. So without realizing it, we sit tensely, muscles grabbing in bunches at the head, neck, or back – as if by holding tight we can hold tomorrow. A white-knuckle grip on the telephone or the steering wheel, restless pencil-tapping or twisting, turning insomnia – all can be symptomatic of the unarticulated sentiment: if I stand guard, I can govern the future.

The truth in that statement can be sifted out and the stress left behind. First, there is no certainty that all will be well at any time. Second, the tension in your body, the result of your mental struggle, serves no helpful purpose. In fact, it's counterproductive. Lastly, there *is* something you can do about the future; you can plan for it. Lastly, you can learn to pace yourself so that most of what you want to happen will. Most important of all is a positive, cooperative attitude toward time.

PACE YOURSELF FOR PEACE.

Time Expanders

Instead of tangling time with negative attitudes which cause stress and promote defeat, expand time by thinking positively and using time productively. Take the following example.

> *Time Tangler:* I'll never finish this project by 3:00 p.m. – there's not enough time!
> *Time Expander:* The project can be broken down into separate tasks.
> I can delegate some parts and have the work completed in time.

Another way to pace yourself is to get into the habit of planning. Always organize your chores in priority order. You probably already know that. But before attacking the chore list, you often lose valuable time in wheel-spinning – time that robs you of a peaceful pace, leaving important work to pile up at the end of the day. To avoid this pitfall of procrastination, keep this key phrase close by:

START! MAKE A BEGINNING!

Maybe the reason you put off beginning is that your list is unrealistically long. Setting attainable goals – a "do-able" list – is important. Check your list against another key phrase: "Make an ending." If you can't draw a line on a day's work, you are back in the perfectionist trap, trying to do Everything.

Remembering that no one, not even Super You, can do it all, learn to distinguish between what *has* to be done and what you'd like to get done. And learn to delegate. Many people feel that if they want something done right, they have to do it themselves. Doing it all yourself doesn't allow you to spend enough time on the truly important tasks – the ones only you can do. By delegating you may lose some of your control, but you'll also gain by getting the lion's share of the work done and by sharing the experience with others.

DON'T PROCRASTINATE, DELEGATE!

At work, give away tasks that don't require your minute-to-minute involvement. If you're at home with your child, let him or her put away the laundry. So what if the towels aren't folded exactly your way? The chore is done and your child feels good about helping.

As for volunteer activities, learn to turn down at least some of the requests for your freebie time – the pleas for fund-raising, telephone-canvassing, bazaar-baking, or speech-making. "Good works" done in anger (grumpily: "Why did I ever say I'd do this?") do nothing for you, and perhaps not much for the cause you're supposedly helping. This is not to undermine your social conscience or your sincere desire to be of some small help to humanity, but only to temper your good intentions with good sense. A rule for wise planners and pacers: Save your time and energy for the extracurriculars that demand your own special talents, and let others do what *they* can do equally well or better than you.

SAY YES ONLY TO WHAT YOU DO BEST. YOU CAN'T DO IT ALL; LET THEM DO THE REST!

Also, take a few minutes every morning to plan. Arrange your tasks in the most efficient order. Whether at home or at the office, make all your phone calls at one time. If you have three errands in different parts of town, think of the most time-saving sequence for doing them. If one errand is not essential, put it off until another day. Travel and shopping are easier at certain times, so stay out of the snarl of rush-hour traffic if possible. By carefully matching hours to tasks, you can get more done in less time and avoid putting undue pressure on yourself.

ARE YOU MARKING TIME OR MAKING THE MOST OF IT?

These Future Pacers are small economies aimed at conserving as much time and energy as you can.

Dealing with Different Timetables

You who are time-possessed or at least highly organized will find it incredibly frustrating to be kept waiting or to stand by and watch someone else waste your time.

If your mate is slower than you are in getting ready for an important event, one way to handle the situation is to mark the calendar with a time that's considerably earlier than the specified hour of arrival (gauge this by how late your spouse usually runs).

Another way to avoid being caught in a time trap is to let it be known ahead of time that you prefer to go on ahead and meet there, instead of missing the beginning of a play, meeting, church service, or whatever. When you're dressed, merely announce that you are ready – and then go!

A healthy practice in a business setting is to express your feelings about being on time. When making an appointment or arranging to meet for lunch, just a simple sentence works very well: "I'm on a tight schedule and only have an hour today. Do you think that will be enough time?" The other person now knows your feelings and also has a heightened awareness of the need to be prompt.

Parents whose tempers and tongues are worn out from hurry-upping young dawdlers would do well early on to teach respect for time. A child who is marching to a very slow drummer may have to miss a carpool or a Scout meeting or two in order to understand that unmet schedules mean lost opportunities. You too will profit from any such lessons which help your child take charge of being on time; you'll be much less time-tense if you're managing just your own timetable, not everyone else's besides.

DON'T WASTE YOUR PRIME TIME WORRYING ABOUT OTHERS BEING ON TIME.

A Gift of Time

Every week treat yourself to a bonus hour or two. Set your wake-up alarm an hour early or go to sleep an hour late. Use this time to indulge yourself in some pleasurable activity, something strictly for fun which you can look forward to. Don't force yourself to earn it or deprive yourself if you haven't done all you were "supposed" to do. When you're pacing yourself, plan for pleasure too.

A GIFT OF TIME IS A TIMELESS GIFT.

CONCERNED? OR WORRIED SICK?

When it comes to sources of worry, there is an endless well-spring. Besides the typical and relatively simple concerns such as, "Will Junior ever get his act together and pass algebra?" or "Where will the money come from to pay for Christmas?" the news furnishes us with grist for our anxiety mills on a stress-by-the-hour basis.

In between televised game shows, soaps, and sports, we are kept up to date on the latest potential hazards: pesticides, carcinogens, nuclear holocaust, world hunger, guerrilla warfare, inflation, unemployment *and,* to top off all this gloom-and-doom, the ill effects of stress!

A firm perspective is required to keep your bearings in the swirling crosscurrents of today's fearful possibilities. To cope with this burden, it is important to define just what you're worrying about. Someone once said that if you're like most people, 40 percent of your time is spent worrying about things that never happen; 30 percent is spent fretting about things that can't be changed by all the worry in the world (old decisions that can't be reversed, for instance); 12 percent of your worry time is over misinterpreting the feelings of others; and 10 percent is over your health, which only gets worse when you worry! That leaves about 8 percent for legitimate concerns – which takes us back to where we started: Will Junior pass algebra? And where will the Christmas money come from?

Too often you are bumped along by the current of the day's activities without taking time to identify the niggling apprehension that has your teeth on edge. Stop where you are and label that elusive feeling of uneasiness: "I am worried." Now you're getting somewhere! Next, name what it is you're worried about. If you acknowledge that your worry falls into a category beyond your control, most of the uncomfortable emotion will dissipate with that understanding.

Let's assume for now that your cause for concern is legitimate. The next question to answer is: "Is my worry producing a solution?" One very common, very honest response would be, "No, but it gives me something to do." This statement leads to two key concepts.

First, worry isn't something you do, it's something you feel – it's the stress factor. When you divide out the stress, the quotient is concern. Concern is the equivalent of caring and that *is* something you can do. That's the second key concept. Now you can go to work.

Write down *what* you can do about the situation and *when*. Make the *what* a step-by-step action plan. By noting *when,* you can tell yourself to set aside your concern until that time.

The following simplified formula is an antidote to worry:

Face your fears.
Find the facts.
Take action.

A final step to minimizing the feelings of worry and fear is to share them with someone in your support system – friend or family member. As one young child confided to her mother, "It's too much work to worry alone."

However skilled you become in your stress management, there still will be times when, although matters are out of your hands, worry persists – and truly you wouldn't

be human if it didn't. Coping with the anxiety of waiting up for a teenage driver who's out long past curfew will pressure the best stress manager. Staying relaxed is not even normal while awaiting news from a hospital emergency room. Prayer is a great comforter at these times. Some agree that the best thing you can do for your mind and body at moments like these is *move*. One person describes cleaning the house at top speed, proceeding through the familiar, comforting routine, but accomplishing the work in half the usual time.

In the Still of the Night

Whatever else you do about worry, don't add to the stress by berating or belittling yourself for it. Worry is part of human nature, especially in the middle of the night. That's when you're most vulnerable to going over and over the same issue without finding any solution. Fitful sleep is exhausting and frustrating, but it is also forgivable. This is important to understand. So universal is this human experience that Napoleon once said that 3:00 a.m. courage is the rarest kind. Matthew J. Culligan, author of *How to Avoid Stress Before It Kills You,* noted that in Scandinavia the time between 4:00 and 5:00 a.m. is called the "hour of the wolf," when "nameless dreads, ghosts of the past, and fears of the future sneak up on the subconscious."

When this kind of stress encroaches on your rest, don't lie there and listen to your heart beat – meditate. Or get up and read, sew, clean the garage, write a report.

When periods of this kind of insomnia plague you, be prepared. Sometimes when your daytime hours are overloaded, your inner alarm goes off too early in the morning and sets you to remembering details from the day before and getting ready for the day ahead. Keep a pad and pencil on the nightstand. If your sleep is disturbed by persistent thoughts, rouse up and record them. Once they're safely jotted down, your brain can let go and return to rest.

The Worry List

One technique to get a handle on your troubles is to write them down. Check around the edges of your consciousness carefully so that you have a complete catalog of your worries. That way none will be left floating around, vying for attention, causing problems. Date the list and file it. A week from today get out the list. How many of these itemized concerns are you still worried about? Wait another week and do this again. Repeat the process in a month or so. Save the list to review next year. What will this procedure show you? Probably that not much was worth worrying about. Most items on your list will disappear within a few days. In a week, month, or year, you probably will forget them altogether. Funny how they seemed so important at the time!

When, at some future time, a difficult situation arises and you find yourself expecting that the *best* will happen, instead of the worst, pat yourself on the back. You have made great strides in less-stress living.

PLUG INTO THE POWER OF POSITIVE EXPECTATION.

Plan for Your Wakefulness

Another way to outwit the restless night-watcher in you is to plan ahead for those wakeful hours. And make your plans pleasant ones. Buy a new magazine or get that book you've been wanting to read. Set it out where you'll be able to read without disturbing anyone else. Put a blanket close by so you'll be comfortable when you get up. Chances are, with your restless time thus secured, you'll sleep right through the night. If you don't, at least you have something to look forward to.

Change the Channel

A trick for getting a child out of the grips of a nightmare is to pretend the pillow is the screen of a television set. The bad dream the child is "watching" is on one side of the pillow. When the child turns the pillow over, he or she can change the channel to a new show.

Adults are just as apt to have fretful dreams, reeling possible disasters into the wee hours like 1945 "B" movies. Furthermore, chronic worriers seldom rehearse "happily ever after" endings. When you are literally losing sleep over negative, fearful imaginings, flip your pillow over and envision a new scenario with a positive script playing before you.

Worried Sick?

As our society becomes increasingly sophisticated, scientists have found more and better ways of proving much of what our grandparents passed down to us in the form of folk wisdom. The expression, "He worried himself sick," is an apt example. Now most standard medical texts attribute 50 to 80 percent of all diseases and disorders to psychosomatic or stress-related origins – ulcers, high blood pressure, hay fever, arthritis, headaches, impotence, and insomnia, to name a few.

After contracting tuberculosis before there were medicines for it, noted psychologist Rollo May concluded, "When disease strikes, it's often nature's way of saying, 'You must change your life.'" All too often we do just that – wait for disaster to strike before we re-order our lives, if it isn't too late. A better idea would be to make a common-sense accounting now.

Exercise, fun, friends, family, a good job – the keys to a happy life are also the ingredients to a healthy life. Dr. George Vaillant of Harvard believes that the best protection against today's major illnesses is good mental health. The cornerstones for contentment have been summed up in three simple, profound components. What a person needs is . . .

> something to do,
> someone to love,
> something to look forward to.

Money, Money, Money

Money, honestly earned, can be the source of much satisfaction. It can buy education, more time with your family, or more leisure for creative pursuits. But your perspective about money may determine the tension you feel. For example, financial worries figure high among life experiences that are stress-producing.

Sages and cynics have philosophized for centuries about financial stress:

Money doesn't always bring happiness.
People with ten million dollars are no
happier than people with nine million.

Hobart Brown

That money talks I'll not deny.
I heard it once. It said good-bye.

Richard Armour

Money won't buy happiness, but it will
pay the salaries of a large research
staff to study the problem.

Bill Vaughan

If you make money your god,
it will plague you like the devil.

Henry Fielding

In order to break through the stress associated with money, separate the issues into three. Are you worried about:

havig enough money for your needs?
having enough money for the extras?
having enough money to keep up with the Joneses?

Working two jobs to keep food on the table can be heroic, but working nights to cover payments on a sports car, especially when your family is at home and wishing you were there, becomes a question of priorities.

In an old Russian short story, "How Much Land Does a Man Need?", the peasants of a village were given one day to stake out new lands for themselves. All they had to do was walk around the perimeter of the new territory and be sure to return by dusk. Propelled by ambition, the greedy protagonist tried to walk around too much land and, when he returned, died of exhaustion.

The folk lesson is pertinent today. In a materialistic culture, money buys things which become symbols of self. So it's easy to get off balance – buying on credit, borrowing too much, living beyond your means and under constant financial pressure.

A good exercise is to list the most important or satisfying aspects of your life. Now look at the list and put a dollar sign by those which can be bought. The bottom-line punch line to this exercise is simply that money provides for surprisingly few of our needs. Money won't buy a beautiful relationship, health or a long life... or fresh snow to ski on... or the colors of spring... or summer sun to snooze in. Life can be plentiful if you plan well, spend wisely, and live within your stress comfort zone.

DOLLARS DON'T BUY LIFE'S DEEPEST DELIGHTS.

PEOPLE WHO NEED PEOPLE

When a clerk in a store moves like a tortoise or chatters to a friend on the phone while you wait, the stress you feel is easy to deal with because you have some clear-cut options – taking your business elsewhere, for example.

But when your mate watches television while you're trying to tell about your day, your child waits until bedtime to announce that there's an important assignment due tomorrow, or your best friend is getting married and you find it out from someone else first – the stress takes on special feelings because you have close relationships with these people. On one hand, support from family and friends plays an invaluable role in diminishing the ill effects of stress. On the other, stress occurs most where you expect it least – with those you love.

This paradox shouldn't be surprising. Naturally you have more intense feelings, both bad and good, for a person you're close to than for a stranger. The key is in the word *expect*. In any relationship, how realistic your expectations are is in direct proportion to how much stress you will feel.

Twosomes

No relationship is as fantasized or romanticized as the love between man and woman – husband and wife, lovers, partners, mates. The ideal of someone who can love you as you are, someone who can share your dreams and fears, can be real. But a relationship without stress can't. The scene of the candlelit supper for two, complete with violin music and fountains of fresh roses, is at best misleading. "People don't live together that way, except on holiday. Rather they are at close quarters, where they can see each other's pimples, wrinkles, and sags," says Herbert G. Zerof, author of *Finding Intimacy*. "The dream must be relinquished in order to enjoy the real thing."

Having realistic expectations doesn't mean that we sit around and wait for conflict. Rather, when conflict happens, we accept it as part of the natural rhythm of a close relationship and treat it as such, something which comes and goes. Alan Alda, star of movies and television, wrote of his own longstanding marriage, "The good times come in waves."

Author Judith Viorst confessed in her article, "Sometimes I Hate My Husband," that "seasons of love give way to seasons of hate...and seasons of hate give way (if only we can hang on and hold out) to seasons of love."

Understanding that conflict does occur leads to an attitude of "We'll ride out the storm," rather than "Our relationship has sunk."

HOLD ON FOR DEAR LIFE. HOLD ON, DEAR, FOR LIFE.

Just Between Us

Airing differences between the two of you in reasonable discussion beats suppressing anger or avoiding issues until a real blow-up occurs.

Set aside a time, at least once a week. Agree on a topic and then take ten minutes to talk about it. Or, as Marriage Encounter recommends, write to each other in that ten-minute time period instead. Writing carries no tone of voice and is far less likely to be loaded with accusatorial barbs that slip out during conversation. Also, the tension level of the exchange is lower. But whether you talk or write, be careful to *express how you feel rather than what you think your partner "should" do.* The purpose is not to make one person right or wrong, but to share and understand each other's feelings and, in the process, grow together.

"Selective Insensitivity"

Even the most perfectly suited couple can eventually drive each other crazy if the little irritations are allowed to loom too large in their life together. He litters the floor with his socks. She leaves her curling iron on too long. Anyone in a twosome can fill in the blanks. He does _____. She does _____. And so on.

You've probably noticed that nagging not only doesn't work but develops into bickering. "I would if you would…" And around and around it goes, in a never-resolving circular conversation.

Dr. Lois Leiderman Davitz talks about avoiding domestic squabbles through "selective insensitivity," that is, ignoring those irritations that aren't worth creating problems over. To help sort through the emotions which surround issues, Dr. Davitz suggests these three questions to ask yourself: Is this issue life-threatening? Is it worth making a fuss over? Will my life change if I get to the bottom of this?

Clarifying your own motives is another equally important consideration. Check your intention. Are you more interested in changing the annoying behavior or proving your partner wrong? Imagine how you'd feel with the socks picked up or the hot curler cool. Do you still have an urge to prove a point to your partner? You're probably playing the heads-I-win-tails-you-lose game. Nobody scores in this one! General peevishness which can come with proximity rarely gets your partner to pay off with, "Ah, yes. You're right and I'm wrong."

In any case, practicing "selective insensitivity" – choosing to ignore minor bad habits – goes a long way toward smoothing out what might otherwise be a rocky, or at least pebble-strewn, road.

WHOSE BAD HABIT AM I STUMBLING OVER?

A Dual Deal

The two-career couple is commonplace now and often neither of the two principals is entirely comfortable in her or his new role. How to cope? By negotiating and sharing responsibilities and most of all by learning to compromise. Working couples offer these stress-reducing maxims:

Divide up the household chores. Allow for preferences. Perhaps one of you truly prefers cleaning to cooking. If there is one least favorite chore for both of you, alternate it every week.

Communicate your sexual needs. But be prepared to meet your partner halfway.

Support your mate. A healthy interest in and respect for each other's workday pursuits make for constructive give-and-take conversations at day's end. Successes should be praised, ungrudgingly, and setbacks discussed with sympathy and understanding.

DIVIDE (THE RESPONSIBILITIES)
AND CONQUER (THE STRESS).

Parenting = Pressures

To say that parenting is stressful is a laughable understatement. Keeping your parental expectations realistic is essential but extremely difficult because so many feelings crowd and cloud the issues.

One of the most damaging of parenting's perpetual myths is that parents should control their children. In a very real sense they can't, for no human being can control another. Trying to potty train a toddler gives an inkling of power struggles to come in later years; there's no way on earth to train a two-year-old until he's ready! When your third-grader's spelling grades slip, you can sit her down at a desk with a book, but you can't force the learning.

When a parent's illusion of control is dispelled, fear usually follows. But then, if you stop to think about it, you are left with all you really had in the first place: influence, teaching, love, and limits.

At no time is it more important to keep an identity of your own (to say nothing of a buoyant sense of humor) than as a parent. Then, with whatever energy is left, follow the best advice you can find.

Former President Harry S. Truman declared, with wit and practicality, "I have found the best way to give advice to your children is to find out what they want, and then advise them to do it."

Two more cardinal rules for less stressful parenting: First, let your children handle as much responsibility as they can. From this they learn trust, independence, and self-esteem. Second, say "yes" whenever you can. This makes any important "no's" more emphatic.

White Flags

When the heat of battle rages over every emotionally charged domestic detail, wave a white flag. Declare a temporary truce to relax as a family group and move toward less stress. Structure some family time – one or two hours a week – away from the "outside world" (peer groups, telephone, and television). Choose an activity that fits your family. For some it may be a Sunday night supper, when children of all ages can settle down and settle in. Take the phone off the hook. Set the table with place mats and flowers from the garden or the corner flower-seller. Light a votive candle or two, a pleasant ritual which adds peace to the occasion. Absolutely no television. No controversial conversation. Just family being together.

If a mealtime gathering doesn't work, how about a drive in the car? Don't try to settle grievances or correct faults. Just enjoy the scenery and let the conversation drift benignly and easily. Other White Flags might be a family picnic or a swim. Each family needs to find its own White Flags – times of truce to relieve build-ups of stress.

List Talk

To minimize the stress between parent and child, a most effective method is List Talk. If you as a parent have gripes to communicate or chores to request, make a list and post it where it can't help but be seen – on the bathroom mirror or the bedroom door. Let your child know the list is in lieu of bugging, but is not to be ignored. Include a time for completion or compliance to avoid unnecessary confrontation.

Two-way Friendships

Good friends help make life rich and full. And even though the dynamics of friendships are different from those in family relationships, it's important to keep your expectations on target with friends too.

Everyone wants a friend to count on, but it's too much to expect of a friend to be there for you all the time. Not that people are apt to be fair-weather friends, but rather, as Merle Shain said in *When Lovers Are Friends,* "You can only get from a person what he or she has to give."

That grammatical enigma, *a friend in need is a friend indeed,* never did specify whose "need" it is – yours or the friend's, and therefore stands as a verbal monument to two-way friendship. The ultimate truth is that no one friend can fill all your needs all the time.

Maximize the Positive

To have good friends, be a good friend. Concentrating on doing things for others is a Stress Breaker with big benefits. When you are bent on helping someone else, you are less centered on self, and self is where the stress is.

Boost another's self-image with a genuine compliment.

Have some fun. Laugh when you can. When people ask how you are, they aren't asking for a replay of a Russian tragedy with you in the role of redeemed-through-suffering victim. Details of your last ill-starred romance, petty office affairs, or a run-down of your private grocery-list of worries is not the kind of conversation that keeps people coming back for more.

But do disclose your true self. Don't live in a fortress. Allowing friends to share with you on an emotional level is an important part of caring for and about each other.

Telephone Therapy

Tapping into your support system by telephone is a handy Stress Breaker. Keep a book of your close friends' phone numbers. You will be a welcome visitor-by-phone if you are sensitive to your friend's timing. "Got a minute to talk?" is a good way to begin. You can't expect much conversation if your friend is in the tub, getting supper for in-laws, or otherwise preoccupied at the other end. Trade off in your supporting roles; make it clear that you'll be ready to listen when your friend needs to talk to *you*.

Reassuring Remembrances

You probably haven't made a scrapbook in years. Nevertheless, now's the time to make one. People need people; people also need the strength and serenity that can come through other people's words. Gather together words of wisdom which are special to you – lines from favorite poems, quotations, greeting cards with lovely verses and loving signatures. Include remembrances of your roots – advice from grandparents, words of support from friends and relatives. Cut and paste or type – it doesn't matter. Photographs are fine too. What you have in this treasured collection are the symbols and reminders of your support network or stress shield – especially your family and friends.

Browsing through your book of Reassuring Remembrances you will feel the power of others' love. Your own convictions will be strengthened by the philosophies you share with others. And the support of others will energize you for the tasks ahead.

Say Yes to Yourself

How others feel about you is very often a reflection of how you feel about yourself, but expectations are crucial here too. You can't expect to please everybody all the time.

Sometimes saying "no" to others is saying "yes" in a vital way to yourself. Saying "no" is seldom easy because we're all afraid of seeming negative. But "no" can be positive when it frees you to do what's most beneficial to you and others. Too many "yeses" may mean that you're trying to seduce others into liking you by trying to be who they want you to be. Have faith that they will like you even better for who you are.

Let your instincts guide your actions. And when you feel it's right to say "no," expect to feel the slight stress of guilt the first few times. Changing old patterns feels uncomfortable. But it will get easier, and your truthfulness will enable your friends in turn to be more direct with you – to say "no" when *they* need to.

When someone asks you to give up time you can't spare, say "no," then explain why.

> **STRESS IS WHAT TOO MANY "YESES" LEAD TO. SAY "YES" WHEN YOU CAN AND "NO" WHEN YOU NEED TO.**

More Strength, Less Stress

Being assertive is a Stress Breaker too. Your insecurity over your judgments, decisions, or contributions doesn't feel good. You're probably afraid that you won't be listened to, won't be taken seriously, or might even be wrong.

The way to change this anxious behavior is to take risks. Next time you have an idea or opinion, speak up. The more you assert yourself, the more you lose the stress of keeping the real you undercover (while somebody else voices your idea!).

Assertion doesn't have to be verbal. You can assert your own views by silently encouraging others. An approving look can offer praise to a friend in a group. A smile can cheer on a performing child. Just being attentive to your spouse at a company dinner is tacit support.

"To expose your feelings is to risk exposing your true self . . .
But only a person who risks is free."

Anonymous

LETTING GO WITH LOVE

Impromptu interviews with people on the street might elicit frivolous off-the-cuff answers to the question, "What do you want most out of life?" "Tom Selleck." "Brooke Shields." "Eternal youth." "A million dollars." When pressed to be serious, though, most people would likely say, "Happiness" (or the equivalent).

Embittered by a bellicose wife, Mark Twain became pretty cynical by the end of his life. He concluded that "sanity and happiness are an impossible combination." Whether or not you agree with this statement depends on your point of view – and your definition of happiness. Is happiness really an irrational state? Or do you make the mistake of expecting too much? Do you wait to consider yourself happy until there is *no* possible cause for unhappiness left in your life?

Learning not to wait – that is, learning to be happy *in spite of things, not because of things,* has a snowball effect. Positive attitudes generate positive happenings. Dr. Kenneth Pelletier admonishes us not to underestimate the power of mood and expectation.

**BE POSITIVELY EXPECTANT.
DECLARE YOURSELF HAPPY TODAY.**

Break the process of happiness into parts and pieces to better understand it. First subtract unpleasant physical sensations which, as Dr. Christian Schriner points out, account for about 90 percent of what we call unhappiness. So reducing stress is an essential part of the process of becoming happy.

Second, subtract the need to control. Anthropologist Margaret Mackenzie notes: "We are a culture nearly addicted to individual control." This, of course, produces double-bind stress when the faulty logic leads to "I need to control everything, including the uncontrollable." The resolution of this need-to-control kind of stress comes with "letting go." Letting go means releasing yourself from the irrational struggle to control what no one can.

Once released from this trap, you are free to focus on other steps toward serenity.

Letting go also involves surrender, stepping down from your mythical throne. Not only can you not do Everything yourself, you are not in charge of Everything either! This sort of surrender is not an admission of weakness, but an acceptance of reality. And what a relief to realize that you don't always have to flex your muscles and tax your brain to make things happen!

Letting go of the stressful need to control opens you to the calming presence of the loving order of the universe. Some people call this presence God. Others call it a Higher Power. Whatever the words, the power is the same. Getting in touch with this presence is a spiritual experience. Staying in touch is the most powerful stress-reliever of all!

ALLOW THE PRESENCE OF PEACE IN YOUR LIFE.

Sounds of Silence

"Peace is not something you can force on anything or anyone – much less upon one's own mind," observed Dr. Gerald May. "It's like trying to quiet the ocean by pressing down on the waves."

You can, however, put yourself in a place where peace is possible.

Just listening to silence is a good start. Noise is an insidious intruder in our lives. Studies show that most domestic arguments begin when there is a high noise level in the house. And notice your own feeling of lightness and relief when a noisy machine or appliance shuts down.

Wayne E. Oates talks about "nurturing silence in a noisy heart" in his book with the same title. Eternal avenues to this kind of silence are meditation and prayer. Select a quiet place where you can be alone. Settle comfortably in a chair or couch, propped with pillows so that muscle tension is gone. Feel the physical sensation of deep relaxation. Slowly allow your mind to cease its frenetic dashing about from subject to subject as you repeat a mantra (a simple word or phrase) or the beginning of a prayer. Try to spend several minutes in this quietness. For some meditators, this experience will bring heightened spiritual awareness, often through feelings of universality or "connectedness." For others, it is enough just to find tranquility in the stillness.

SET ASIDE A TIME FOR SILENCE.

Break of Day Stress Breaker

Set the alarm and get up earlier than necessary. This may seem an outrageous suggestion, but once you experience the delight of being up alone at dawn, before the onslaught of the day's activities, schedules, and demands, it just may become a habit.

This pale, precious hour may be the only time you'll have all day to be alone, free from distractions, to enjoy your own quietness of mind – time to meditate or pray. This is not just a good – but a great – way to start a day.

Giving your spiritual self time to grow allows you to find that peaceful place in the center of you and prepares you to reach for it in times of need.

When your soul awaits in silence, stress is gone.
With love, you can simply let it go.

God grant me the serenity
to accept the things I cannot change,
courage to change the things I can,
and wisdom to know the difference.

The following test was developed by psychologists Lyle H. Miller and Alma Dell Smith at Boston University Medical Center. Score each item from 1 (almost always) to 5 (never), according to how much of the time each statement applies to you.

1. I eat at least one hot, balanced meal a day.

2. I get seven to eight hours sleep at least four nights a week.

3. I give and receive affection regularly.

4. I have at least one relative within 50 miles on whom I can rely.

5. I exercise to the point of perspiration at least twice a week.

6. I smoke less than half a pack of cigarettes a day.

7. I take fewer than five alcoholic drinks a week.

8. I am the appropriate weight for my height.

9. I have an income adequate to meet basic expenses.

10. I get strength from my religous beliefs.

11. I regularly attend club or social activities.

12. I have a network of friends and acquaintances.

13. I have one or more friends
to confide in about personal matters.

14. I am in good health
(including eyesight, hearing, teeth).

15. I am able to speak openly
about my feelings when angry or worried.

16. I have regular conversations with
the people I live with about domestic problems,
e.g., chores, money and daily living issues.

17. I do something for fun at least once a week.

18. I am able to organize my time effectively.

19. I drink fewer than three cups
of coffee (or tea or cola) a day.

20. I take quiet time for myself during the day.

To get your score, add up the figures and subtract 20. Any number over 30 indicates a vulnerability to stress. You are seriously vulnerable if your score is between 50 and 75, and extremely vulnerable if it is over 75.

Vulnerability Scale from the *Stress Audit* by Lyle H. Miller, Ph.D., and Alma Dell Smith, Ph.D., Boston University Medical Center, © 1983, Biobehavioral Associates. Used by permission of the authors.

SAMPLE STRESS LOG

SITUATIONS	BODILY REACTIONS
My son got hit with a baseball.	*My hands were sweaty and I had a stomach ache.*

NAME YOUR STRESS AND YOUR STRESS BREAKER

EMOTIONAL STATES	STRESS BREAKERS USED
I was fearful.	*Deep breathing and picturing my son playing baseball with friends.*

97

Helene Lerner

Helene Lerner, a native New Yorker, has a deep commitment to finding ways of living more serenely in our high-stress society. Although she is a full-time executive with the *New York Times,* she finds extra hours to carry out her avocation – helping people in community groups and in the corporate workplace reduce their levels of stress.

She graduated Phi Beta Kappa and magna cum laude from Hunter College, earned an M.A. in education from City College of New York, and is now working toward an M.B.A. degree at Pace University. Her strong interest in theater and communication began early, even before she attended the High School of Performing Arts in New York City.

Formerly on the faculty of the New School for Social Research, she is the author also of *Exec-U-Stress.* She is a member of the Association of Training and Development and of Women in Communication.

Roberta Elins

Roberta Elins heads her own public relations agency based in New York. She and her husband own and race thoroughbred horses. With beauty expert Jerome Alexander, she also has authored a do-it-yourself beauty guide called *Be Your Own Makeup Artist.*

Pete Bastiansen

Pete Bastiansen is an award-winning advertising art director and an illustrator, designer, and writer. Except for three years as a television animation artist in Hollywood, he has always lived and worked in Minneapolis – in the advertising agency business, in a partnership called Mom's Art Shop, and now on his own. With characteristic whimsy, he created the name of his present firm, Abercrombie & Bastiansen, and his mythical partner, to feel less alone in his solo operation.